Contents

What are worms?

Worms have long, thin soft bodies.

Worms are long and thin. They are called invertebrates. Invertebrates means that they do not have **backbones**. Worms have very soft bodies. Their head is rounded and their tail is more pointed. Worms do not have legs.

There are four main groups of worm. In each group there are hundreds of different kinds of worm.

Take-Off! Bug Books

WORM

Jill Bailey

Heinemann LIBRARY

First published in Great Britain by Heinemann Library
Halley Court, Jordan Hill, Oxford OX2 8EJ
a division of Reed Educational and Professional Publishing Ltd.
Heinemann is a registered trademark of Reed Educational & Professional Publishing Limited.

OXFORD MELBOURNE AUCKLAND
IBADAN JOHANNESBURG GABORONE
PORTSMOUTH NH CHICAGO BLANTYRE

Designed by Celia Floyd
Illustrations by Alan Male
Printed in Hong Kong/China

04 03 02 01 00
10 9 8 7 6 5 4 3 2 1

ISBN 0 431 01661 5
This book is also available in hardback (ISBN 0 431 01656 9).

British Library Cataloguing in Publication Data

Bailey Jill
Worm. - (Bug books) (Take-off!)
1.worms - Juvenile literature
I. Title
592.6'4

Acknowledgements

The Publishers would like to thank the following for permission to reproduce photographs: Ardea London Ltd: JP Ferrero p5, P Morris p4; Bruce Coleman Ltd: F Labhardt p10, Dr F Sauer p5, K Taylor p22; FLPA: G Hyde pp14, 20, M Rose p12, M Thomas p25; Garden Matters: K Gibson p24, J Phipps p27; Chris Honeywell p28; NHPA: D Woodfall p7; Oxford Scientific Film: K Atkinson pp21, 29, J Cooke pp15, 26, B Davidson p11, C Milkins p13, R Redfern p23, H Taylor p19, D Thompson pp8, 9, 16, 17, 18

Cover photographs reproduced with permission of Oxford Scientific Films/J Cooke

Our thanks to Sue Graves for her advice and expertise in the preparation of this book.

Every effort has been made to contact copyright holders of any material reproduced in this book. Any omissions will be rectified in subsequent printings if notice is given to the Publisher.

For more information about Heinemann Library books, or to order, please telephone +44 (0)1865 888066, or send a fax to +44 (0)1865 314091. You can visit our website at www.heinemann.co.uk

Any words appearing in the text in bold, **like this**, are explained in the Glossary

saddle

A worm makes mucus to help it slide through the soil.

A worm has a swollen part around the middle of its body. This is called the **saddle**. The saddle makes a slippery slime called **mucus**. The mucus helps the worm to slip easily through soil. In this book we are going to look at earthworms.

Where do worms live?

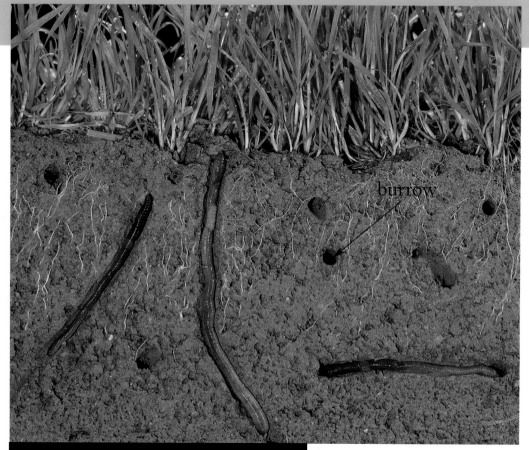

burrow

Worms live in burrows like these.

Worms live in **burrows** in soil. Usually they live near the surface. In very dry or cold weather they may tunnel deeper than the height of an adult. A worm burrow is about as wide as a pencil.

A worm can burrow through 2.5 tonnes of soil in a year – that's nearly the same weight as a female elephant!

A pile of garden soil as high as you may contain 20 worms. The same size pile of soil from old grassland may contain more than 700 worms!

Wild grassland, like this, will have many worms.

What do worms look like?

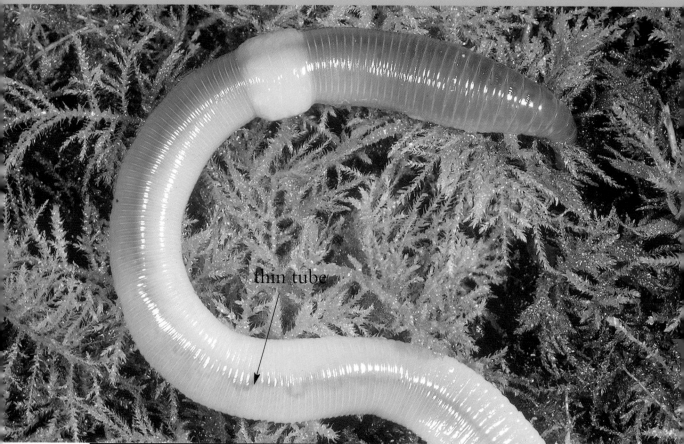

thin tube

A thin tube carries blood around a worm's body.

A worm has no eyes or ears. Its whole body can feel light and sound and it can taste. Can you see a long, thin tube running down this worm? The tube carries red blood along the worm's body.

A worm's body is made up of many parts called segments. Each segment has a few small, stiff **bristles** that act like tiny hooks. The bristles grip the sides of the **burrow** to pull the worm along.

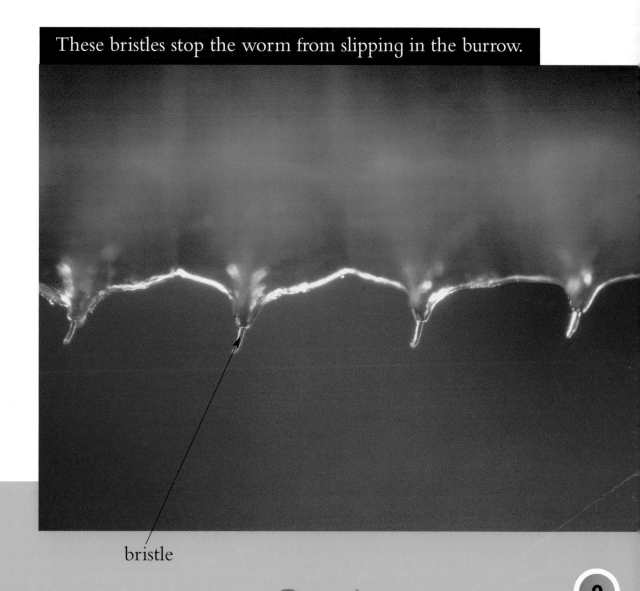

These bristles stop the worm from slipping in the burrow.

bristle

How big are worms?

Earthworms can be different sizes.

Some earthworms are small. A small earthworm can be as long as your finger. Other earthworms can be long. A long earthworm can stretch from your fingertips to your elbow. The smallest kind of earthworm is only as long as your fingernail.

The biggest earthworms in the world can be the length of four adults lying end to end. They can be as wide as two fingers side-by-side.

This is a very long earthworm!

The largest earthworms can be found in Africa and Australia.

What do worms do?

This worm is pushing its way through the soil.

Earthworms spend most of their time underground.
They push their way through soil. If the soil is too
hard to push through the worm will eat its way
through instead.

A worm has dragged these leaves into its burrow.

burrow

Worms like to keep their bodies damp all the time. During a hot day they stay underground. But on warm, damp nights worms may come to the surface of the soil. They drag dead leaves down into their **burrows** to eat.

How long do worms live?

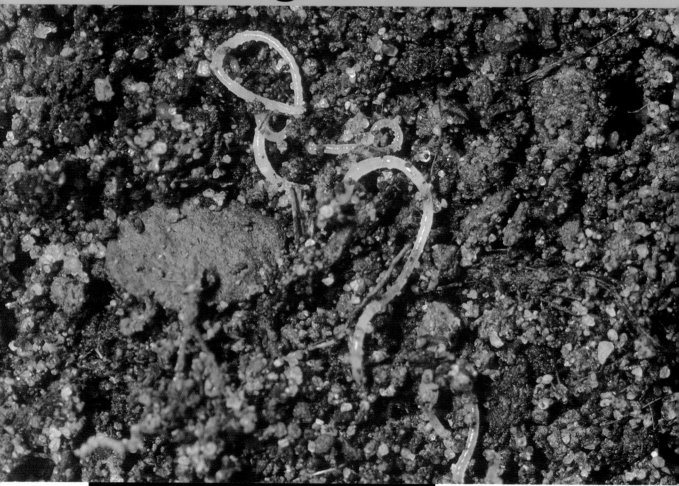

This baby worm is less than a year old.

A worm has to be about one year old before it can have babies. Worms can live for quite a long time. They can live for about eleven years.

You can tell that a worm is an adult when you can see its **saddle**.

Worms use their bristles to cling on to their burrows.

A worm uses its **bristles** to cling hard to its **burrow**. If a bird tries to pull it out, the worm's body may break in half. Sometimes one half grows back into a worm.

How are worms born?

Worms lie side-by-side to mate.

On warm, damp summer evenings, worms come out of their **burrows** and lie side-by-side to **mate**. Each worm gives its partner a drop of special juice. This will help eggs to grow.

Each worm makes a **cocoon** to lay its eggs in. The worm makes the cocoon from thick slime made in its **saddle**. The slime hardens into a cocoon for the eggs.

A worm makes a cocoon from thick slime which then hardens.

How do worms grow?

The cocoon protects the egg until it is ready to hatch.

A worm may lay up to twenty eggs inside each **cocoon**. Many eggs are laid but usually only one of them survives. The egg is protected by the cocoon until it is ready to **hatch**.

18

The baby worm is ready to hatch out of the cocoon after one to five months. The baby worm is very tiny. It stays hidden in the soil.

A baby worm takes at least a year to grow as big as its parents.

What do worms eat?

Worms eat parts of dead plants and animals that they find in the soil.

Worms eat parts of dead leaves and plants that they find in the soil. They eat parts of dead animals that they find too. Worms also eat the soil as they tunnel.

They **grind** down the soil to get at its food. The useless grains of soil pass out of the worm's tail end. Sometimes the waste soil makes small heaps.

This small heap of waste soil is called a worm cast.

worm cast

Which animals attack worms?

This bird has found a worm to eat.

Worms have many enemies. Birds, mice, hedgehogs, badgers and other animals feed on worms. All these animals listen for the sound of the worm moving beneath the surface. When they hear the worm moving they dig it up.

Worms have enemies underground too. Moles dig tunnels through the soil to look for worms. Moles cannot see in the dark, but they can hear and smell well.

This worm has fallen into a mole's tunnel.

How are worms special?

Worms make soil good for growing plants.

Worms are very important to farmers and gardeners. They break down dead leaves by eating them. The breaking down of the dead leaves puts important **minerals** back into the soil. These minerals help to make plants grow.

When worms dig through the soil they mix it up. Their **burrows** let air and rain into the soil. This keeps the soil good for growing plants.

These worms are helping to keep the soil light and airy.

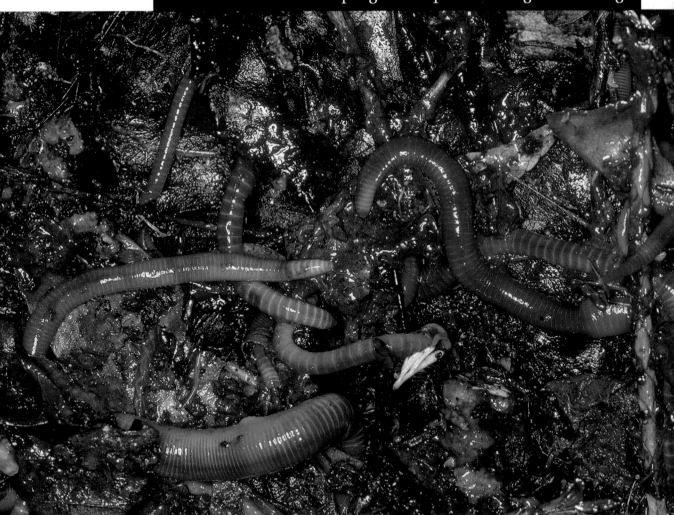

How do worms move?

First the worm stretches out its front end to make it long and thin.

The worm's soft body is filled with a watery liquid. The worm can squeeze its body into different shapes. To move forward, the worm makes its front end long and thin.

Next, the worm pulls its tail end forward.

Then it digs its **bristles** into the ground and pulls its tail end forward. Now it digs in the bristles on its tail and lets go of the front ones as it stretches forward again. And so on.

Thinking about worms

Do this experiment to see how a worm changes shape:

1   Fill a balloon almost full of water.

2   Tie up the end of the balloon so it doesn't leak.

3   Squeeze the balloon. It will get long and thin just like a worm does.

Use a balloon filled with water to see how a worm changes shape.

A **wormery** is a good way to study how worms move through the soil. Now you have read about worms can you answer these questions?

1   What will the worm use the leaves for?

2   How has the worm made its **burrow**?

3   How does the worm get rid of the soil it digs out?

The worm in this wormery is pulling leaves into its burrow.

Bug map

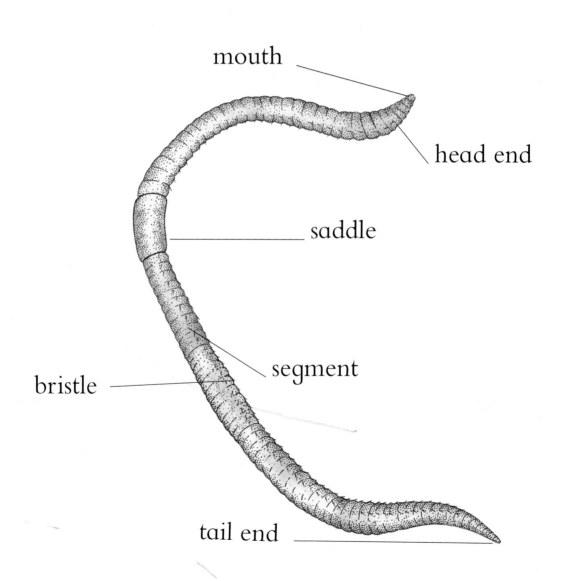

mouth

head end

saddle

segment

bristle

tail end